HAL•LEONARD

pro Vocal
BETTER THAN KARAOKE!

FOR FEMALE SINGERS
VOLUME II

Disney's
B E S T

W9-BDL-173

CONTENTS

Disney Characters and artwork © Disney Enterprises, Inc.

WONDERLAND MUSIC COMPANY, INC.
WALT DISNEY MUSIC COMPANY

ISBN 978-1-4234-0112-4

DISTRIBUTED BY

HAL•LEONARD®
CORPORATION
7777 W. BLUEMOUND RD. P.O. BOX 13819 MILWAUKEE, WI 53213

In Australia Contact:
Hal Leonard Australia Pty. Ltd.
4 Lentara Court
Cheltenham, Victoria, 3192 Australia
Email: ausadmin@halleonard.com.au

Visit Hal Leonard Online at
www.halleonard.com

Beauty and the Beast

from Walt Disney's BEAUTY AND THE BEAST
Lyrics by Howard Ashman
Music by Alan Menken

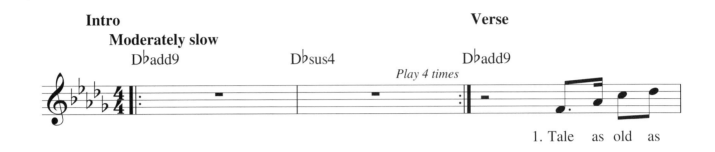

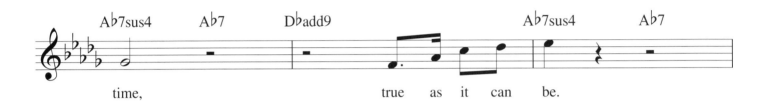

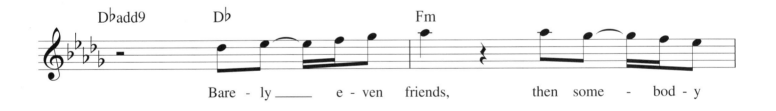

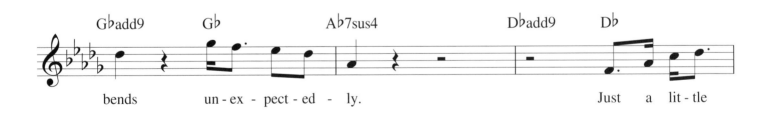

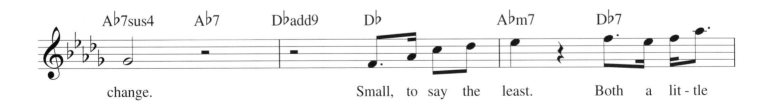

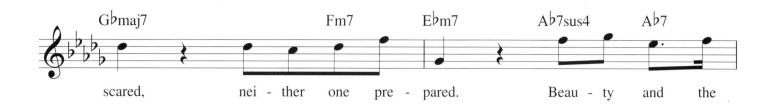

scared,   nei - ther one pre - pared.   Beau - ty and the

Bridge

Beast.   Ev - er just the same.

Ev - er a sur - prise.   Ev - er as be -

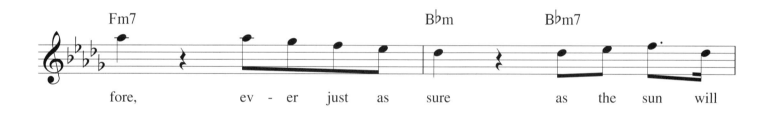

fore,   ev - er just as sure   as the sun will

Verse

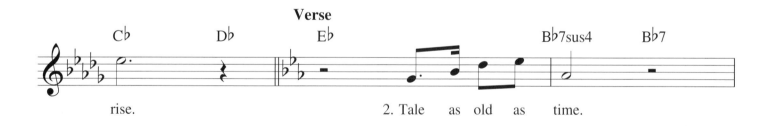

rise.   2. Tale as old as time.

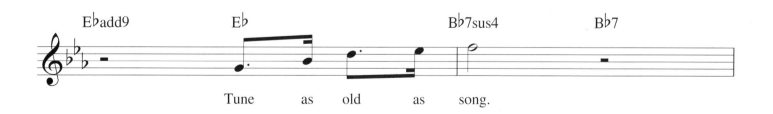

Tune   as old   as song.

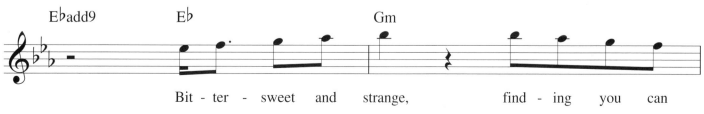

Bit - ter - sweet and strange,   find - ing you can

3

change, learn - ing you were wrong.

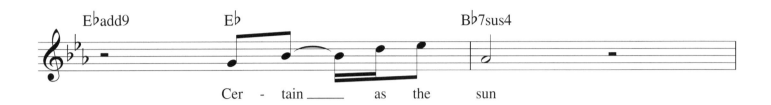

Cer - tain ___ as the sun

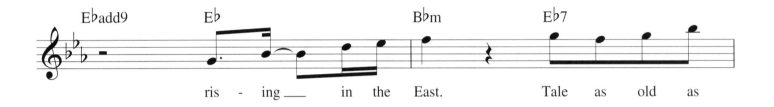

ris - ing ___ in the East. Tale as old as

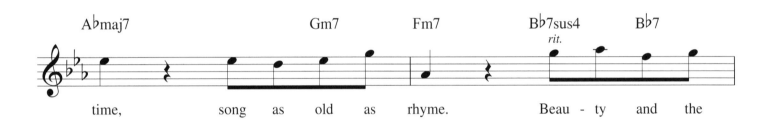

time, song as old as rhyme. Beau - ty and the

A tempo **Slower** **Outro**

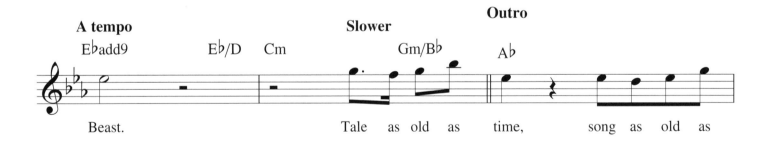

Beast. Tale as old as time, song as old as

A tempo

rhyme. Beau - ty and the Beast.

Candle on the Water

from Walt Disney's PETE'S DRAGON

Words and Music by Al Kasha and Joel Hirschhorn

Intro
Moderately slow

1. I'll be your can-dle on ___ the wa-ter,

my love for you will al-ways burn. I know you're

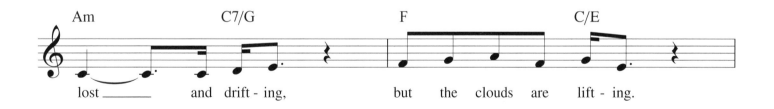

lost ___ and drift-ing, but the clouds are lift-ing.

Don't give up; you have some-where to turn. ___

Verse

2. I'll be your can - dle on ___ the wa - ter,

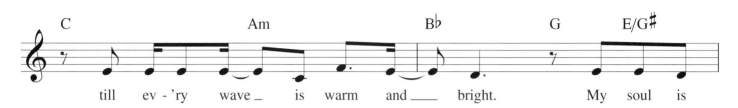

till ev - 'ry wave ___ is warm and ___ bright. My soul is

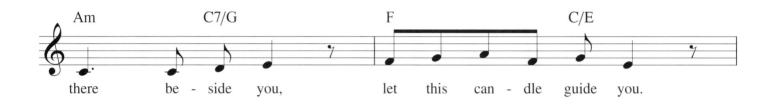

there be - side you, let this can - dle guide you.

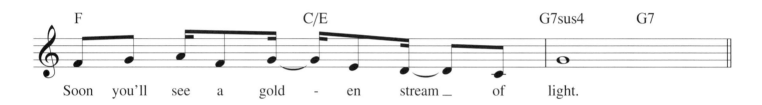

Soon you'll see a gold - en stream ___ of light.

Bridge

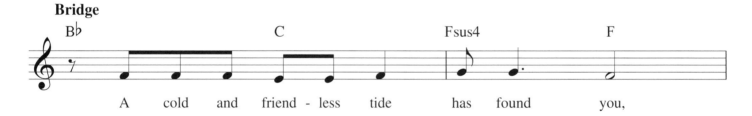

A cold and friend - less tide has found you,

don't let the storm - y dark - ness pull you down.

I'll ___ paint a ray of hope a - round ___ you,

cir - cling in the air, light - ed by a prayer. ___

Circle of Life

from Walt Disney Pictures' THE LION KING
Music by Elton John
Lyrics by Tim Rice

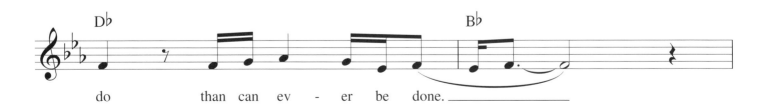

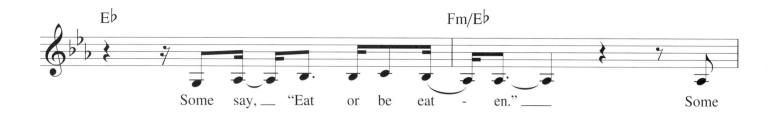

Some say, __ "Eat or be eat - en." __ Some

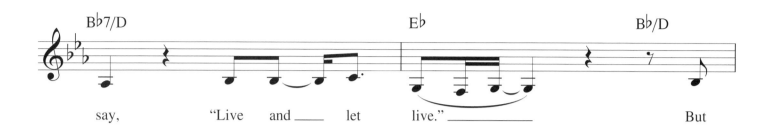

say, "Live and ___ let live." _____ But

all are a - greed, __ as they join the stam - pede, ____ you should

nev - er take more __ than __ you give ___ in the cir - cle __ of life. __

Chorus

It's the wheel of ___ for -

- tune. _____ It's the leap _____ of __ faith. __

It's the band _____ of __ hope _____

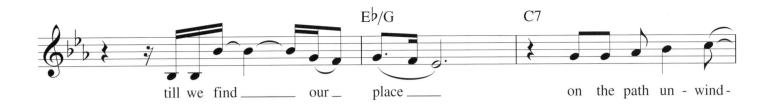

till we find _____ our _ place _____ on the path un-wind-

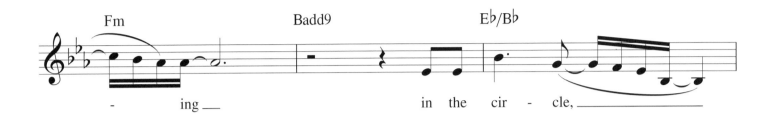

-ing _____ in the cir - cle, _____

the cir - cle _____ of _____ life. _____

Verse

2. Some _____ of us fall by the _____ way - side, and

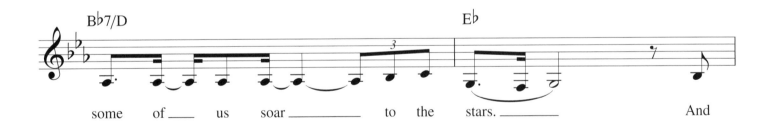

some of _____ us soar _____ to the stars. _____ And

some of _____ us sail _____ through our trou - bles, _____ and

some have to live _____ with the scars. _____ There's

far too __ much __   to take in __ here, __   more to

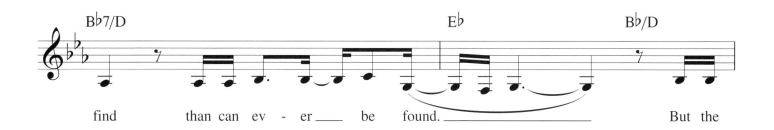

find   than can ev - er __ be found. _____   But the

sun roll - ing high __   through the sap - phi - re sky __ keeps great and small __

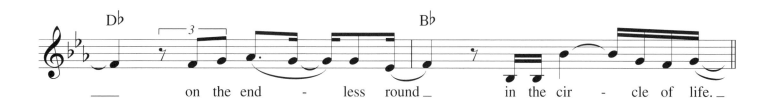

__ on the end - less round __ in the cir - cle of life. __

Chorus

_____   It's the wheel of for - tune. _____

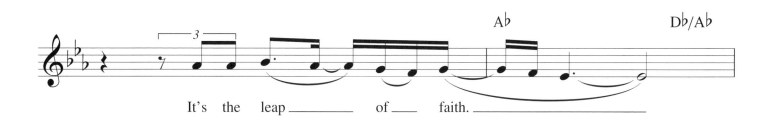

It's the leap _____ of __ faith. _____

It's the band _____ of __ hope _____   till we find our __

place _____ on the path un - wind - ing ___

To Coda ⊕

in the cir - cle, _____

D.S. al Coda

___ the cir - cle ___ of ___ life.

⊕ **Coda**

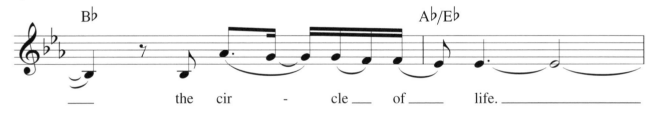

___ the cir - cle ___ of ___ life. _____

___ On the path un - wind - ing _____

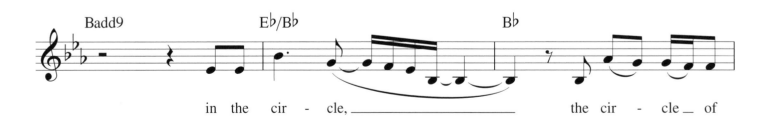

in the cir - cle, _____ the cir - cle __ of

life. _____

Colors of the Wind

from Walt Disney's POCAHONTAS

Music by Alan Menken
Lyrics by Stephen Schwartz

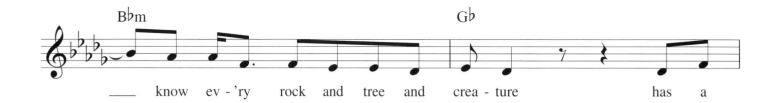

_____ know ev -'ry rock and tree and crea - ture has a

life, has a spir - it, has a name. You

think the on - ly peo - ple _____ who are peo - ple are the

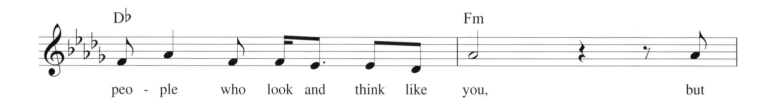

peo - ple who look and think like you, but

if you walk the foot - steps _____ of a stran - ger you'll learn

things you nev - er knew, _ you nev - er knew. Have you

ev - er heard the wolf _____ cry to the blue corn moon, or

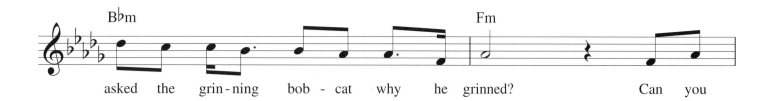

asked the grin-ning bob-cat why he grinned? Can you

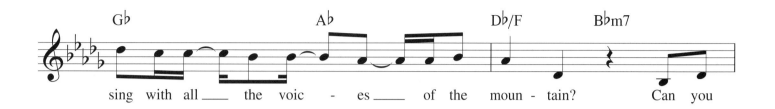

sing with all ___ the voic - es ___ of the moun - tain? Can you

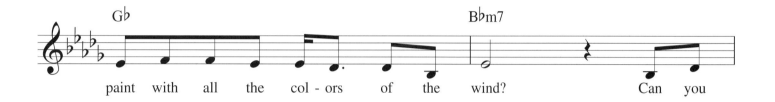

paint with all the col - ors of the wind? Can you

A tempo

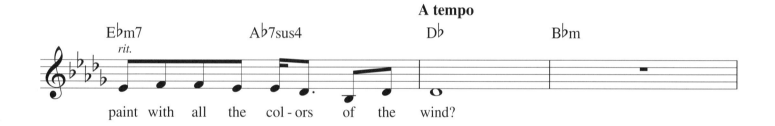

paint with all the col - ors of the wind?

Verse

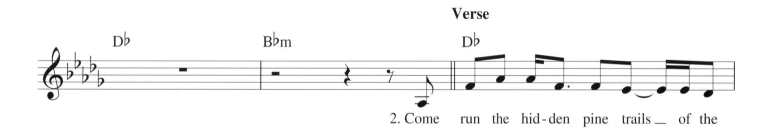

2. Come run the hid-den pine trails _ of the

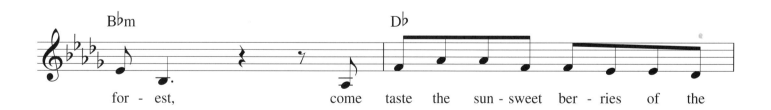

for - est, come taste the sun - sweet ber - ries of the

earth; come roll in all the rich - es all a -

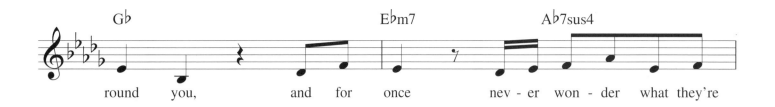

Gb   Ebm7   Ab7sus4

round you,   and for   once   nev - er won - der what they're

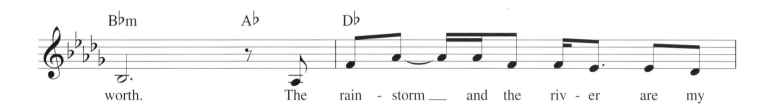

Bbm   Ab   Db

worth.   The rain - storm ___ and the riv - er   are   my

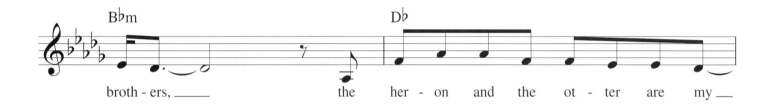

Bbm   Db

broth - ers, ___   the her - on and the ot - ter   are   my ___

Fm   Bbm

___ friends. ___   And we are all con - nect - ed ___ to each

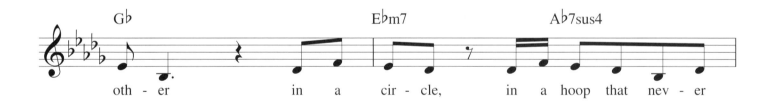

Gb   Ebm7   Ab7sus4

oth - er   in a   cir - cle,   in a hoop that nev - er

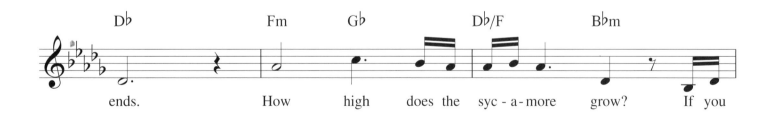

Db   Fm   Gb   Db/F   Bbm

ends.   How high does the syc - a - more grow?   If you

Cb   Ab7sus4   Ab7   Ab7sus4 Ab7 Ab7sus4 Ab7

cut it down,   then you'll nev - er know. ___   And you'll

Outro-Chorus

nev - er hear the wolf __ cry to the blue corn moon, for

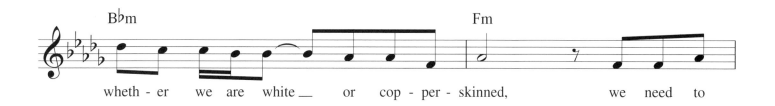

wheth - er we are white __ or cop - per - skinned, we need to

sing with all the voic - es of the moun - tain, need to

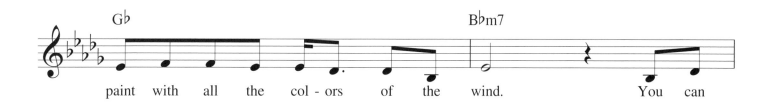

paint with all the col - ors of the wind. You can

own the earth and still all you'll own is earth un - til you can

A tempo

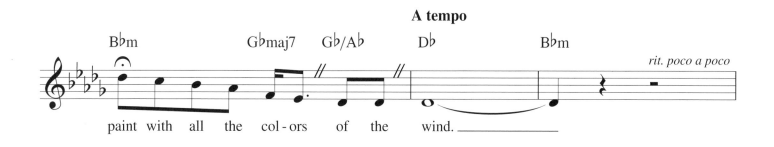

paint with all the col - ors of the wind. _____

17

God Help the Outcasts

from Walt Disney's THE HUNCHBACK OF NOTRE DAME

Music by Alan Menken
Lyrics by Stephen Schwartz

Slowly

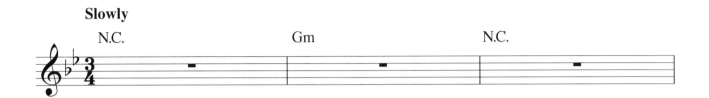

Faster

I don't know if You can

hear me or if You're e - ven there.

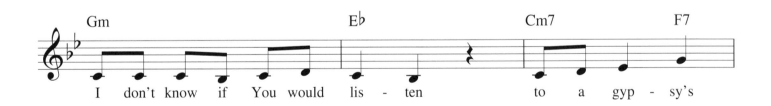

I don't know if You would lis - ten to a gyp - sy's

prayer. Yes, I know I'm just an out - cast, I

should - n't speak to You. Still I see Your face and

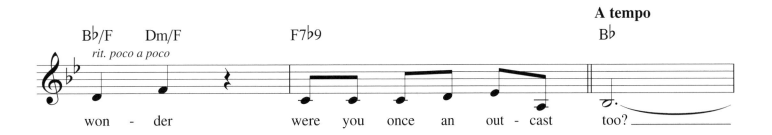

won - der were you once an out - cast too? _____

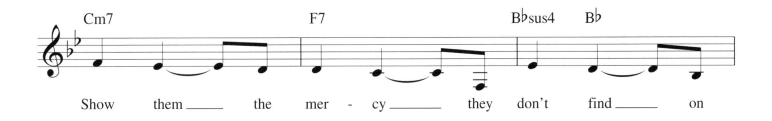

_____ God help _____ the

out - casts, hun - gry from birth.

Show them _____ the mer - cy _____ they don't find _____ on

earth. God help _____ my peo - ple, they

look to You still. God help _____ the

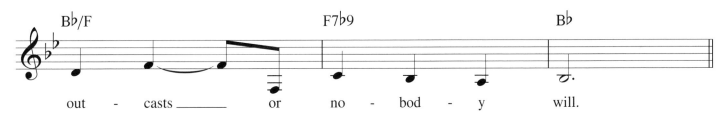

out - casts _____ or no - bod - y will.

I ask for wealth. I ask for

fame. I ask for glo - ry _____ to

shine on _____ my name. _____ I ask for

love _____ I can pos - sess. _____

_____ I ask for God and His an - gels to

bless me. _____

I ask _____ for noth - ing. _____ I can get

by, but I know _____ so man - y _____ less

luck - y than I. Please help ____ my

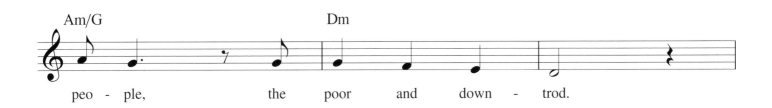

peo - ple, the poor and down - trod.

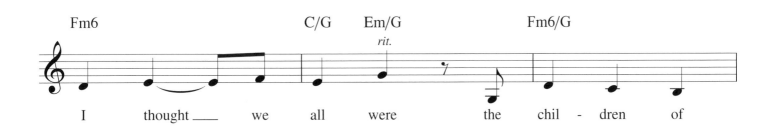

I thought ____ we all were the chil - dren of

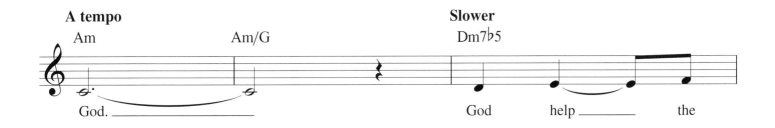

God. ____ God help ____ the

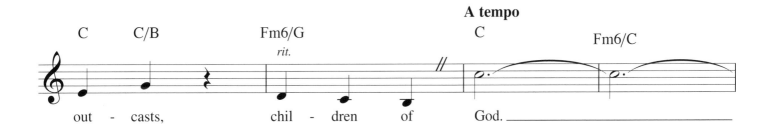

out - casts, chil - dren of God. ____

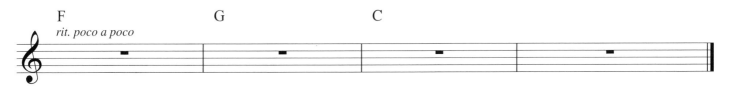

Part of Your World

from Walt Disney's THE LITTLE MERMAID
Lyrics by HOWARD ASHMAN
Music by ALAN MENKEN

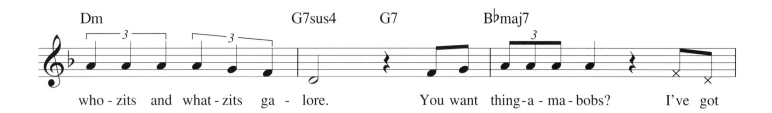

who-zits and what-zits ga-lore. You want thing-a-ma-bobs? I've got

Slower

twen-ty, but who cares? No big deal. I want more. _____

Tempo I

_____ I wan-na be ____ where the peo-ple are.

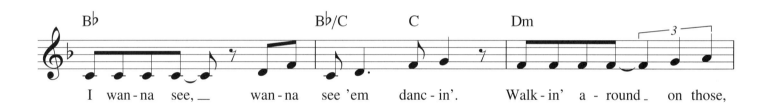

I wan-na see, ____ wan-na see 'em danc-in'. Walk-in' a-round ____ on those,

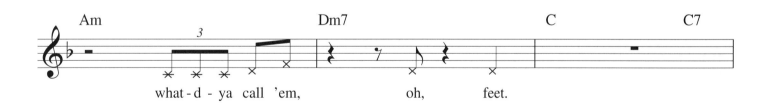

what-d-ya call 'em, oh, feet.

Flip-pin' your fins, ____ you don't get too far. ____ Legs are re-quired ____ for

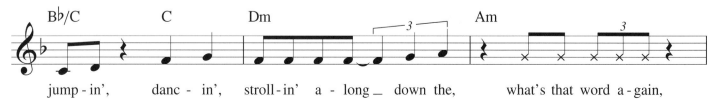

jump-in', danc-in', stroll-in' a-long ____ down the, what's that word a-gain,

street. _____ Up where they walk, up where they

run, up where they stay all day ___ in the sun. Wan-der-in'

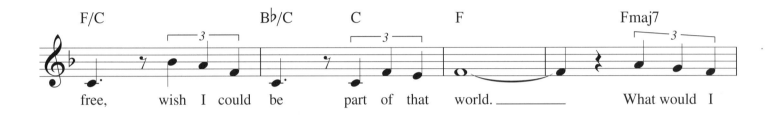

free, wish I could be part of that world. _____ What would I

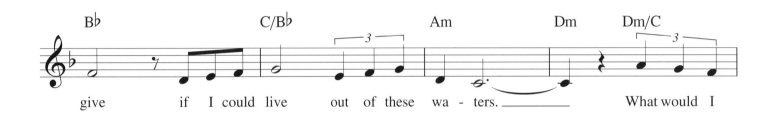

give if I could live out of these wa-ters. _____ What would I

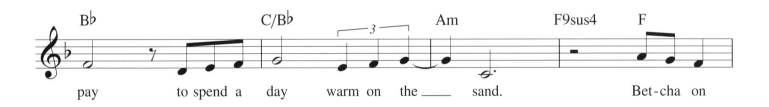

pay to spend a day warm on the ___ sand. Bet-cha on

land they un-der-stand. Bet they don't re-pri-mand their daugh-

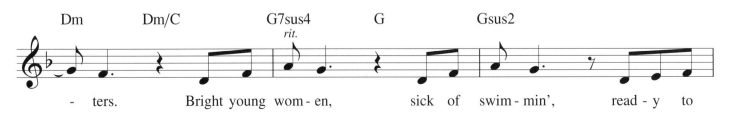

-ters. Bright young wom-en, sick of swim-min', read-y to

Zip-a-Dee-Doo-Dah

from Walt Disney's SONG OF THE SOUTH
Words by Ray Gilbert
Music by Allie Wrubel

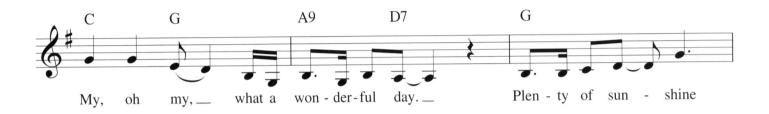

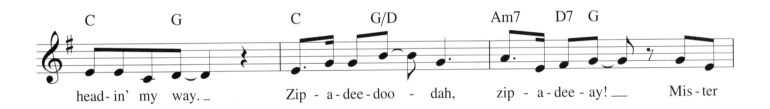

Zip - a - dee - doo - dah, zip - a - dee - ay! ___

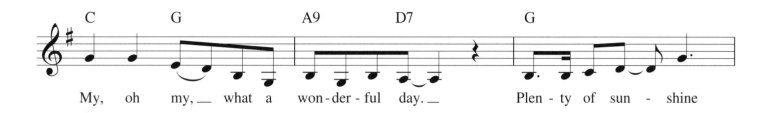

My, oh my, ___ what a won - der - ful day. ___ Plen - ty of sun - shine

head - in' my way. ___ Zip - a - dee - doo - dah, zip - a - dee - ay! ___ Mis - ter

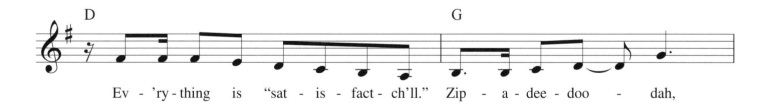

Blue - bird's on my shoul - der. It's the truth, it's "act- ch'll."

Ev - 'ry - thing is "sat - is - fact - ch'll." Zip - a - dee - doo - dah,

zip - a - dee - ay! ___ Won - der - ful feel - in', feel - in' this way. ___

Won - der - ful feel - in', won - der - ful day. ___

You'll Be in My Heart

(Pop Version)

from Walt Disney Pictures' TARZAN ™

Words and Music by Phil Collins

Intro
Moderately

Verse

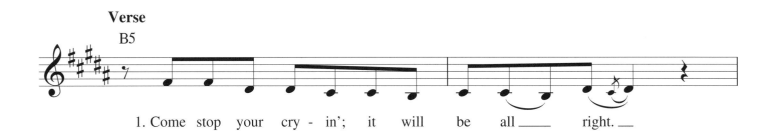

1. Come stop your cry - in'; it will be all ____ right. ____

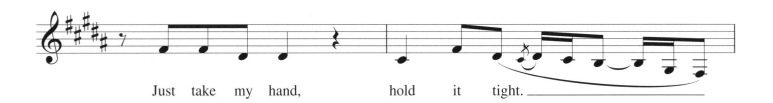

Just take my hand, hold it tight. ____

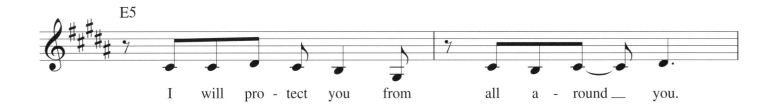

I will pro - tect you from all a - round ____ you.

I will be here, don't you ____ cry. For one so small, you

seem so ____ strong. ____ My arms will hold you, ____ keep you

see in time, I know.

When des-ti-ny calls you, you must be strong. It

may not be with you, but you got-ta hold on. They'll

see in time, I know. We'll

Chorus

show them to-geth-er, 'cause you'll be in my

heart. Be-lieve me, you'll be in my heart. I'll be there from

this day on, now and for-ev-er-more.

You'll be in my heart no mat-ter what they